B

by Iain Gray

PUBLISHING

WRITING *to* REMEMBER

LangSyne

PUBLISHING

WRITING *to* REMEMBER

79 Main Street, Newtongrange,
Midlothian EH22 4NA
Tel: 0131 344 0414   Fax: 0845 075 6085
E-mail: info@lang-syne.co.uk
www.langsyneshop.co.uk

Design by Dorothy Meikle
Printed by Printwell Ltd
© Lang Syne Publishers Ltd 2022

ISBN 978-1-85217-108-7

Brown

MOTTO:
Floreat Majestas
(Let majesty flourish).

CREST:
A lion rampant holding
in it's paw a fleur-de-lys.

Echoes of a far distant past
can still be found in most names

Chapter one:

Origins of Scottish surnames

by George Forbes

It all began with the Normans.

For it was they who introduced surnames into common usage more than a thousand years ago, initially based on the title of their estates, local villages and chateaux in France to distinguish and identify these landholdings, usually acquired at the point of a bloodstained sword.

Such grand descriptions also helped enhance the prestige of these arrogant warlords and generally glorify their lofty positions high above the humble serfs slaving away below in the pecking order who only had single names, often with Biblical connotations as in Pierre and Jacques.

The only descriptive distinctions among this peasantry concerned their occupations, like Pierre the swineherd or Jacques the ferryman.

The Normans themselves were originally Vikings (or Northmen) who raided, colonised and eventually settled down around the French coastline.

They had sailed up the Seine in their longboats in 900AD under their ferocious leader Rollo and ruled the roost in north east France before sailing over to conquer England, bringing their relatively new tradition of having surnames with them.

It took another hundred years for the Normans to percolate northwards and surnames did not begin to appear in Scotland until the thirteenth century.

These adventurous knights brought an aura of chivalry with them and it was said no damsel of any distinction would marry a man unless he had at least two names.

The family names included that of Scotland's great hero Robert De Brus and his compatriots were warriors from families like the De Morevils, De Umphravils, De Berkelais, De Quincis, De Viponts and De Vaux.

As the knights settled the boundaries of their vast estates, they took territorial names, as in Hamilton, Moray, Crawford, Cunningham, Dunbar, Ross, Wemyss, Dundas, Galloway, Renfrew, Greenhill, Hazelwood, Sandylands and Church-hill.

Other names, though not with any obvious geographical or topographical features, nevertheless derived from ancient parishes like Douglas, Forbes, Dalyell and Guthrie.

Other surnames were coined in connection with occupations, castles or legendary deeds.

Stuart originated in the word steward, a prestigious post which was an integral part of any large medieval household. The same applied to Cooks, Chamberlains, Constables and Porters.

Borders towns and forts – needed in areas like the Debateable Lands which were constantly fought over by feuding local families – had their own distinctive names; and it was often from them that the resident groups took their communal titles, as in the Grahams of Annandale, the Elliots and Armstrongs of the East Marches, the Scotts and Kerrs of Teviotdale and Eskdale.

Even physical attributes crept into surnames, as in Small, Little and More (the latter being 'beg' in Gaelic), Long or Lang, Stark, Stout, Strong or Strang and even Jolly.

Mieklejohns would have had the strength of several men, while Littlejohn was named after the legendary sidekick of Robin Hood.

Colours got into the act with Black, White, Grey, Brown and Green (Red developed into Reid, Ruddy or Ruddiman). Blue was rare and nobody ever wanted to be associated with yellow.

Pompous worthies took the name Wiseman, Goodman and Goodall.

Words intimating the sons of leading figures were soon affiliated into the language as in Johnson, Adamson, Richardson and Thomson, while the Norman equivalent of Fitz (from the French-Latin 'filius' meaning 'son') cropped up in Fitzmaurice and Fitzgerald.

The prefix 'Mac' was 'son of' in Gaelic and clans often originated with occupations – as in MacNab being sons of the Abbot, MacPherson and MacVicar being sons of the minister and MacIntosh being sons of the chief.

The church's influence could be found in the names Kirk, Clerk, Clarke, Bishop, Friar and Monk. Proctor came from a church official, Singer and Sangster from choristers, Gilchrist and Gillies from Christ's servant, Mitchell, Gilmory and Gilmour from servants of St Michael and Mary, Malcolm from a servant of Columba and Gillespie from a bishop's servant.

The rudimentary medical profession was represented by Barber (a trade which also once included dentistry and surgery) as well as Leech or Leitch.

Businessmen produced Merchants, Mercers, Monypennies, Chapmans, Sellers and Scales, while down at the old village watermill the names that cropped up included Miller, Walker and Fuller.

Other self explanatory trades included – Brewsters and Brewers, Tailors, Saddlers, Wrights, Cartwrights, Smiths, Harpers, Joiners, Sawyers, Masons and Plumbers.

Even the scenery was utilised as in Craig, Moor, Hill, Glen, Wood and Forrest.

Rank, whether high or low, took its place with Laird, Barron, Knight, Tennant, Farmer, Husband, Granger, Grieve, Shepherd, Shearer and Fletcher.

The hunt and the chase supplied Hunter, Falconer, Fowler, Fox, Forrester, Archer and Spearman.

The renowned medieval historian Froissart, who eulogised about the romantic deeds of chivalry (and who condemned Scotland as being a poverty stricken wasteland), once sniffily dismissed the peasantry of his native France as the jacquerie (or the jacques-without-names) but it was these same humble folk who ended up overthrowing the arrogant aristocracy.

In the olden days, only the blueblooded knights of antiquity were entitled to full, proper names, both Christian and surnames, but with the passing of time and a more egalitarian, less feudal atmosphere, more respectful and worthy titles spread throughout the populace as a whole.

Echoes of a far distant past can still be found in most names and they can be borne with pride in commemoration of past generations who fought and toiled in some capacity or other to make our nation what it now is, for good or ill.

Chapter two:

The French connection

Originally a descriptive term for the colour of a person's hair, complexion, or clothing, Brown is now one of the most common surnames in Scotland, England, and the USA, but there is nothing commonplace about the lives, times, and achievements of those who have borne the name down through the centuries until the present day.

Variations of 'Brown' exist in every European language. In France it is le Brun, and in German Brun, or Braun, while other versions are Bron, Browne, Browyn, Brwne, Brune, Brouin, Broune, and Broun.

The name le Brune ('the Brown') is found in Cumberland only a few decades after the Norman Conquest of England in 1066, at a time when this vast area of the north of England was part of the Scottish kingdom.

This family of le Brune would have been

among those Norman warriors, their families, and retainers who settled in England and later in Scotland following the conquest.

The name also appears in Scotland in 1128 when a Sir David le Brun is recorded as witnessing the foundation charter of Holyrood Abbey.

King David I, according to legend, had been hunting in the grounds of what would later become the abbey and palace of Holyrood, in Edinburgh, when he was saved from a charging stag, and founded the Holy Cross (Holyrood) Abbey in thanks for his salvation.

As a witness to the foundation charter, it is probable that Sir David le Brun was one of the knights who had accompanied his monarch on the hunt.

The most common form of the name in Scotland for a number of centuries was 'Broun', and the infamous Ragman Roll of 1296 records Brouns from Berwick, Linlithgow, Lanark, and Edinburgh as signatories.

Signed by 1,500 bishops, earls, and burgesses such as the Brouns, the roll was a

humiliating treaty of fealty to England's Edward I,
known as the Hammer of the Scots, and is known
as the Ragman Roll because of the profusion of rib-
bons that dangle from the seals of the signatories.

The Brouns, in common with the vast
majority of those who swore fealty to Edward,
had no option but to do so, but avenged
themselves later when they took up the cause
of Scotland's freedom during the bloody Wars of
Independence.

The name is also found towards the close
of the thirteenth century in Fife, Perth, and the
northeast of Scotland, while a family known as
the Brouns of Hartrie are known to have settled
near Biggar, in Lanarkshire, by the turn of the
fifteenth century.

A Clan Broun Society exists today in the
USA, and claims a descent from the family of the
Brouns of Colstoun, in East Lothian.

Such a family did indeed exist and thrive
for centuries in East Lothian and, intriguingly,
claimed a descent from the Royal House of
France.

This is not as improbable as it may seem, because alliances endured for centuries between Scotland and France, and not only on a political level.

The Auld Alliance also embraced alliances through marriage, and it is possible that a French 'le Brun' with close connections to the French monarchy, may have married a daughter of the Scottish aristocracy.

The arms of the Brouns of Colstoun feature the three fleur-de-lys of the French monarchy, while their crest is a lion holding a fleur-de-lys in its paw. Keeping up the tradition of a royal pedigree, their motto is 'Let Majesty Flourish.'

One colourful tradition of the Brouns of Colstoun concerns a strange fruit known as the Colstoun Pear, which was said to have been imbued with magical properties by the thirteenth century necromancer and wizard Hugo de Gifford of Yester, in the Scottish Borders.

Reputed to ensure prosperity for the family who owned it, the Colstoun Pear became the property of the Brouns of Colstoun in 1543 when George Broun married Jean Hay, a daughter of Lord Yester.

The pear was Jean Hay's precious dowry, and is said to have retained its ripe freshness right up until the end of the seventeenth century when a pregnant descendant, craving a taste of the out-of-season fruit, treated herself to a bite.

The pear immediately lost its magical properties and became rock hard.

The pregnant lady's whim, however, does not appear to have adversely affected the subsequent fortunes of the Brouns of Colstoun. In 1686, Patrick Broun of Colstoun is recorded as being created a baronet of Nova Scotia (New Scotland).

This title appears to have been inherited, because James VI had granted the first baronetcies of Nova Scotia in 1624 to Scots of substance who were willing to invest in what was Scotland's first attempt to establish a colony in North America.

The area for proposed colonisation took in not only present-day Nova Scotia but also New

Brunswick and the territory between there and the St. Lawrence River.

Nearly forty Scottish magnates, including a Broun, were granted allotments of territory and, although not physically required to take up possession of their distant new lands, a special ceremony was enacted on the Castle Hill of Edinburgh where a small area was designated 'Nova Scotia' to allow them to formally take 'possession' of their land and be duly honoured with their baronetcy.

Nova Scotia, in effect, had been 'incorporated' into the Scottish kingdom, while the scheme marked the introduction of the honour of baronet to Scotland.

A combination of factors, including the terms of a peace treaty between England and France, led to the colony finally being abandoned in 1632.

The right to the baronetcy was retained, however, along with the provision that the title would pass to male heirs.

Their spirit of commercial enterprise was

not dampened by the failure of the colonisation project, and branches of the Brouns of Colstoun subsequently settled as successful merchants in Elsinore, in Denmark, where the name is still to be found.

Chapter three:

Kinsmen of the clansmen

The Brouns, or Browns, are also heir to colourful traditions with roots in the mists and mountains of the Highlands and Islands.

The name has it equivalent in the Gaelic 'donn', or 'duinne', while a common form is Mac-Mhaoil-Dhuinn, or Mac-Ghille-Dhuinn, meaning 'son of the brown devotee, servant, or lad.'

Other forms of the name include McIlduin and McIldyn.

A common misconception, however, is that the Gaelic Mac a' bhriuthainn ('son of the brehon') can be anglicised as 'brown'. The name actually stems from Britheamh, which was the honoured title given to the hereditary judges, or lawgivers, of the Western Isles.

There are Browns on both the west coast islands of Islay and Tiree, where they are known

as 'Brunaich', but they are believed to be of
Lowland origin.

A much stronger link between the Browns
and Gaeldom can be traced to the proud clans of
both MacMillan and Lamont.

This link is so strong that Browns who
can trace an origin back to the territorial lands of
either of these clans are entitled to be regarded as
belonging to a sept, or branch, of the clan.

The MacMillans at various times held
lands in Carradale, Knapdale, Loch Tayside,
Lochaber, Glenurquhart, the Outer Hebrides, and
Galloway, and it was the son of a MacMillan of
Carradale who is thought to have been the
progenitor of the 'MacMillan Browns.'

The colourful legend is that MacMillan of
Carradale had three sons who, along with their
father and their clansmen, set off in hot pursuit of
a band of Atholmen who had raided their lands
and driven off their cattle.

A fierce battle ensued after they met up
with the raiders, but the MacMillans emerged
victorious and retrieved their precious cattle.

The younger son, however, pursued the Atholmen off the field of battle and returned to Carradale Glen a few days later bearing a great number of heads of those he had single-handedly slain.

His proud father is said to have cried out: 'My little hero, my brown-haired lad! You're the champion yourself, to master them!"

The descendants of the heroic young son subsequently took the name of Brown and were known as the Mac 'illemhaoil-dhuins, 'the brown-haired MacMillans.'

The power of the MacMillans appears to have gone into decline from about the early seventeenth century, and it is believed many of the 'MacMillan Browns' settled in the Cowal peninsula, where a branch of MacMillans had already settled, and entered into kinship with the Lamont Clan.

The Lamonts had been in the Cowal area of Argyll since at least the early thirteenth century, but the fate of the clan and their kinsmen such as the Browns was sealed in 1646 when they clashed with the powerful Clan Campbell.

A force of Campbells led by Sir Colin Campbell of Ardkinglas besieged the Lamont's Toward Castle and, outnumbered and all but overwhelmed, Sir James Lamont had no option but to surrender in return for the safe passage of his family, clansmen, and kinsmen.

Sir Colin Campbell promptly reneged on the deal, however, and cast Sir James into Dunstaffnage Castle, where he was kept in dark and damp confinement for five years, not even allowed a change of clothing.

A more terrible fate awaited his clansmen and kinsmen, who were also thrown into confinement for about a week and a number of the women raped and killed.

The surviving prisoners were then marched to Dunoon and, adding sacrilege to the crimes already committed, were taken into a churchyard where about 100 of them were either shot, stabbed, or had their throats cut.

Nearly 40 of the leading clansmen were

hanged from the same tree, cut down while still alive, thrown into hastily dug pits, covered with earth, and left to suffocate to death.

Some Lamonts and their Brown kinsfolk managed to not only survive the butchery, however, but were able to thrive through the succeeding centuries.

Those Browns of today who can trace a descent to either the MacMillans or the Lamonts are entitled to adopt the particular clan's crest and motto.

The MacMillan crest features two hands grasping a sword, while the Lamont crest is an upright right hand, palm facing outwards.

The MacMillan motto is 'I learn to succour the distressed', and the Lamont motto, 'Neither spare nor disgrace.'

Brown was also the name adopted by many dispossessed Highland clansmen following the abortive Jacobite Rebellion of 1745, when not only many aspects of an ancient way of life such as the wearing of tartan, the carrying of weapons, and the playing of bagpipes were banned, but the clan name itself was also proscribed.

Outlawed as robbers, the MacGregors are an example of a clan forced on some occasions for the sake of survival to adopt a less controversial or 'neutral' surname, such as Brown, Gray, White, or Smith.

This is understood to have been the case with a humble family of Browns who farmed at Crathie, in Aberdeenshire, and one of whose descendants was to gain fame as Queen Victoria's faithful ghillie, or servant, John Brown.

Chapter four:

Royal retainers and freedom fighters

It was shortly after Queen Victoria and her consort Prince Albert had Balmoral Castle in Aberdeenshire built as their Scottish retreat that the 29-year-old John Brown, who was born in 1826, came to work there from nearby Crathie as a gamekeeper and general estate worker.

He rapidly gained royal favour, becoming Prince Albert's personal ghillie and, following the consort's death in 1861, the personal servant of the queen herself.

Victoria was bereft over the loss of her beloved Albert, and Brown appears to have provided much needed comfort and solace throughout her long years of mourning.

The blunt speaking farmer's son from Crathie was despised by the queen's immediate family, royal courtiers, and other servants who resented and were jealous of the favours the monarch granted him and the easy informality he was allowed to adopt towards her.

Among the many gifts he received from a grateful Victoria were two medals especially created for him, the Faithful Servant Medal and the Devoted Service Medal, while she also commissioned a portrait of her loyal ghillie.

He died at Windsor Castle in 1883, after contracting a chill that could have been averted had he immediately taken to his sickbed. Brown was buried in his native Crathie.

Victoria was inconsolable with grief at the loss of her loyal retainer and had a life-sized statue of him erected in the grounds of Balmoral.

Following her death in 1901, however, the statue was removed to a less prominent spot, while Edward VII set about destroying all other reminders of Brown that he could find.

Speculation was rife during Brown and Victoria's lifetimes as to the exact nature of their close relationship, with whispered rumours that it was of a sexual nature.

The speculation continues to the present day, and was recently refuelled with the discovery of diaries that make the startling claim that the Reverend Norman MacLeod, Victoria's chaplain, had made a deathbed confession that he had reluctantly presided over the secret marriage of the queen to her humble servant.

Doubt has been cast on the veracity of the account committed to the diaries, however, but doubtless the speculation will continue for many more years to come.

Across thousands of miles of ocean from the farm in Crathie where John Brown was born, another John Brown, born in Torrington, Connecticut, in 1800, is revered as the American abolitionist whose militant opposition to slavery lit the spark of the Civil War that eventually freed the slaves.

He had a number of nicknames, including Oswatomie Brown, Old Man Brown, and Captain Brown, and it was as a military leader that he led a raid on the federal armoury at Harpers Ferry, in present day West Virginia, in 1859.

He was captured and hanged, but his memory survives in the song *John Brown's Body*, which became a favourite marching song of the Union troops during the American Civil War of 1861-65.

Other noted Browns include Hablot Knight Brown (1815-82), the English artist who, better known as 'Phiz', illustrated many books including the great novels of Charles Dickens.

Also in the realms of fiction, the weekly escapades of the comic characters *The Broons* have endeared themselves for many years to thousands of readers throughout the world in the Scottish *Sunday Post* newspaper.

P. Hume Brown was a distinguished Historiographer-Royal for Scotland and professor of Ancient (Scottish) History and Palaeography at Edinburgh University.

He was the author of a number of important Scottish historical works, including a popular history of Scotland that has been recently revised and re-published as *Story of a Nation: Scotland – A Concise History**.

Taking to the skies, Sir Arthur Whitten Brown (1886-1948) achieved fame when, together with Sir John Alcock, he made the first transatlantic flight in 1919, crossing from Newfoundland to Ireland.

In the world of contemporary politics, Gordon Brown is the Labour politician who served as British Prime Minister from June of 2007 to May 2010.

Born in Fife in 1951, and Member of Parliament (MP) for Kirkcaldy, he also served from 1997 to 2007 as Chancellor of the Exchequer under Labour Prime Minister Tony Blair.

After lending his considerable and impassioned political weight for a "No" vote in the referendum for Scottish Independence in September of 2014, he announced three months later his retiral from active Parliamentary politics.

*Lang Syne Publishing, Newtongrange

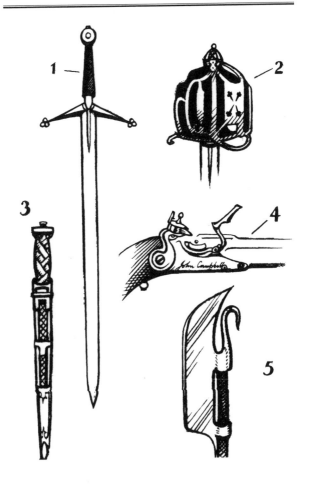

Highland weapons

1)   The claymore or two-handed sword
     (fifteenth or early sixteenth century)

2)   Basket hilt of broadsword
     made in Stirling, 1716

3)   Highland dirk
     (eighteenth century)

4)   Steel pistol *(detail)* made in Doune

5)   Head of Lochaber Axe as carried
     in the '45 and earlier